Love, Coping, and Compassion...

Conquering My Sons Cancer

By: James Craven

Text Copyright 2012
James Craven
All Rights Reserved

Table of Contents

Chapter 1: Week 1(Days 1-6)
Chapter 2: Week 2 (Days 8 & 10)
Chapter 3: Week 3 (Days 21, 23, 26)
Chapter 4: May Update
Chapter 5: June Update
Chapter 6: July Update
Chapter 7: August Update
Chapter 8: The Hardest Question
Chapter 9: "Why Did God Choose Me to Be Sick"
Chapter 10: October Update
Chapter 11: "My Hero"
Chapter 12: December Update
Chapter 13: 11 for 2011
Chapter 14: February Update
Chapter 15: 1 Year Anniversary
Chapter 16: Robby Atherton Foundation Speech
Chapter 17: 2011...A Year in Pictures

ACKNOWLEDGEMENT

This fight wouldn't have been easy if we didn't have such a great support group of family, friends, strangers, and organizations which make up Team Alex.

Rick Hall was the first friend I called when we got the news about Alex. He spread the word very quickly at work. My co-workers at Vesco Oil really out did themselves from monetary donations to picking out a Nintendo 3DS and games for Alex to play while in the hospital and/or at doctor's appointments. I never knew I worked with such a great group of people.

We have some of the greatest friends and neighbors, who early on organized the 1st fundraiser for our family, knowing we were going to need it. Crystal Albensi, Shannon Szpanelewski, and Gina Roy...

you are more than friends you are family.

Ms. Bean and the entire Trinity Lutheran School in Utica, MI showed what it is to be a true Christian. This group took it upon themselves to organize a "Live Strong" day for Alex. They sold a bunch of "I Live Strong for Alex" bracelets to help our family. Thank you doesn't nearly say enough to what it meant to our family.

Kevin Zeoli, my best friend in comedy, took it upon himself to volunteer a Saturday night, which is a prime night for comedy, to organize a comedy show to benefit my family, a true selfless thing to do which is not seen too often in our world of comedy.

So many groups and organizations that do things for the greater good to thank as well. The Moose Lodge in Clinton Township organized a spaghetti dinner and auction.

The Utica/Shelby Rotary extended themselves to do more than what was ever expected.

The Robby Atherton Foundation, who has turned tragedy into triumph not only for our family but for their own as well.

The Knights of Columbus council in Clinton Township who sponsored Alex's "wish trip" to swim with the dolphins and all the theme parks in Orlando, Florida. The trip will always have a special place in our hearts. As well as Ingrid Todt from The Rainbow Connection of Michigan, who made the wish trip possible.

There are so many other groups who did things behind the scenes who didn't want any acknowledgement for the great things they did. Just know what you have done is truly appreciated!

So many selfless acts of kindness from so many people are truly amazing. It's renewed my faith in people. There are those who don't get enough credit for doing great things in this world.

Without every single one of you and many more there would be no Team Alex. We would have been left to fight this battle on our own. We are truly blessed to have each and every one of you in our life.

Our parents, Vince & Merlene Coletti and Ron & Joann Backus, you were there for us when we needed you most. From taking care of Courtney and Ryan to helping us whenever we asked and almost anything we asked, you didn't flinch to help us. It pained us so much to tell you on that awful day…to see the pain and fear in your face was almost too much to bear. You may love us as children but your love is bigger and stronger for your grandchildren.

Courtney and Ryan...the best brother and sister a brother could ask for. You remained strong the entire time and grew up faster than you needed to in the past year. Courtney celebrated every time Alex came home from the hospital. Ryan wanted to save all his money at one point so he could buy Alex a "comfort system bed" so his back wouldn't hurt anymore. Without you two our family wouldn't be as strong as we are today...I love you both so much!

I wouldn't be able to tell this story without the support of my rock...my wife Nancy. You reminded me every day to not look at yesterday....or look to tomorrow...but to live for what today gives me. You will forever be my rock! Thank you and I love you.

Introduction

Large B Cell Lymphoma of the Bone is a rare type of lymphoma. It accounts for 1-3% of all the types of lymphoma. Instead of attacking the organ system it attacks the bones, destroying healthy bones and cells, having them appear moth eaten on scans and x-rays. It causes the bones to become weak and brittle. It's this disease which changed everything in my 12 year old son Alex's life on Monday April 4th, 2011...when we heard one simple word...Cancer.
Being a parent you know your job is to protect your children from being hurt and to know I couldn't was the most hopeless feeling in the world. Thankfully my family and I have a great support system of family, friends, and even strangers who have become essential in helping us through my son's battle. Because of them I have learned so much.

I have learned what strength in numbers truly means while learning to expect the unexpected. I have learned to hate something with every feeling I have, at the same time love more than I ever thought I could. I learned nothing in life is too trivial and what it's like to be inspired. I learned what hopes and dreams are while witnessing the power of prayers.

Most importantly I learned how strong my family is.

From the 1st day I knew I wouldn't always be able to let my feelings show. If I was going to have a bad day it would influence my son's day. I wanted to make sure he had as few bad days as possible. So, I started a chronicle to show my feelings without letting him see how I felt on the inside. It was tough, many of them were written while watching him sleep in the hospital as the meds coursed through his veins and more often than not written through many tears because I couldn't believe this was actually happening.

I know Alex read them, because he started to ask more questions about me and his Mom and our feelings. I think it gave him a better understanding of how a parent struggles and feel's, which made our relationship stronger. He inspired me in more ways than he will ever know.

This is the chronicle of my son's battle with cancer.

Love, Coping, and Compassion...Conquering My Sons Cancer

CHAPTER 1

(Day 1)

April 4, 2011........Just another Monday to most people.
Not to me.....it's the day that changed everything in my life.
In one simple word......Cancer.

I heard the word and.....it wasn't me they were talking about.....it wasn't my father....or grandfather. It was my 12 year old son.
Of all the questions that went through my head in an instant only one stood out
WHY HIM AND NOT ME???
He's just a kid not just that, he's a good kid....honor roll, athlete, great brother, and a wonderful son.
My wife and I were left in a room to try and figure out how do we tell him?
How do we tell his brother, sister and his grandparents?

Somehow through the tears, hug, kisses and 1 million "I love you's" we did.
I didn't sleep a wink last night....I couldn't
Thankfully he did.....with the help of heavy pain relief.
Today I took a mental health day to wrap my head around what lies ahead.
I know he's scared....he knows we are scared....we told each other.
Tomorrow morning we go to Children's Hospital in Detroit....for more scans and tests.
So please keep your fingers crossed, say a prayer, wish some good vibes, or whatever it is you do for good things to happen.
I know this isn't for everyone.....but it's the only way I can cope.....putting words down for me to see how I feel.

(Day 2)

April 4, 2011........Just another Monday to most people.
Not to me.....it's the day that changed everything in my life.
In one simple word......Cancer.

Another restless night of sleep.......it's hard waiting for a day you never want to come.
We knew it had to come......we need answers.
It's scary to know that Alex is going through this.......and he's been brave today.
He heard straight from the doctor what it is inside of him.....what it's done to him.
For 12 years old, he was very adult about it, and even asked a few questions.
He gave his own description of what and where it hurts.....his doctor was very impressed with his details

The many tests have begun.....simple so far...blood work, ultrasounds, and x-rays.
But we know more are coming......Biopsy tomorrow afternoon and a possible PET scan Friday.

Results of the test today are good news/ bad news.....
The good news is..... Lymphoma and Leukemia have been ruled out. It also has not spread to any organs just to the bones....That alone is a ray of hope
There is a slight chance it is a benign form that will still involve treatment.
The bad news......The disease is more extensive than originally thought.....and the doctor has never seen it this widespread before.
Positive thinking and a sense of humor has gotten all of us through today.
I'm amazed at the bravery my son has put forward......and how solid as a rock Nancy has been.

(Day 3)

April 4, 2011........Just another Monday to most people.
Not to me.....it's the day that changed everything in my life.
In one simple word......Cancer

Today was filled with anticipation......for many reasons.
Alex went to school today......he wanted to visit his friends and teachers.
They are all very concerned about him........it shows how much kids actually care for their friends.
It melted my heart to see.

The other anticipated part of the day is Alex's biopsy.
It's just a small surgery......but the results can mean so much.
They are taking a very small part of the bone near his knee......he won't miss it.

The doctor is hoping and has us hopeful it might be benign lesions on his bones.
My hope is he just isn't trying to get our hopes up......because right now I feel pretty good.

Alex showed bravery throughout the surgery process for his biopsy......he admitted he was scared but knows it had to be done.
Now we wait for the results from pathology....thankfully we can do this at home.
But I have to say......waiting truly is the hardest part right now.

(Day 4)

April 4, 2011........Just another Monday to most people.
Not to me it was the day that changed everything in my life.
In one simple word......Cancer

Today was a day of rest.......an easy day compared to the last few.
Alex took it easy....after overdoing things last night because of feeling invincible from the Toradol and Tylenol 3 w/codeine.

His leg hurts from his surgery yesterday....he said "The only good thing about my leg hurting is I don't think about my back hurting."
This kid is tough as nails!!!
I think things are starting to sink in on him; he's been a little moody..... I wish I could peek into his brain and thoughts to know how he is really feeling.

It's a lot for a 12 year old to think about and have on his mind......he asks about some thing's but I don't think all the things he wants to. Maybe over the weekend he will want to talk more about his feelings.....That's on his time table. Nancy and I will be there when he's ready to talk.

There won't be any news over the weekend about his biopsy.....those results will be in Monday afternoon, hopefully,
So for now we wait, worry, and wonder.
Thank you for all your kind words and support......Nancy and I know we are truly blessed with some of the best friends and family anyone could ever ask for.

(Day 6)

April 4, 2011........Just another Monday to most people.
Not to me.....it's the day that changed everything in my life
In one simple word......Cancer

Finally...a normal day.
Alex's pain was controlled much better today....Enough for him to go outside and play with his brother.
It was nice to see him play outside.....even better to see him playing with his brother.
I do have to say....as much as brothers and sister fight/argue.....Ryan and Courtney have been GREAT!!
Ryan has been making sure he is entertaining Alex....one way or another.
Courtney has been working with Alex's teacher to help organize a "Live Strong Day" at school.

Not much is being said about his condition....maybe because there were no doctor appointments, or he/we are a little tired of talking about it for now.
Not really much to report on today.....we are just waiting on Monday.

Thank you all for being great friends and family and your continued support, thoughts, and prayers

CHAPTER 2

(Day 8)

April 4, 2011........Just another Monday to most people.
Not to me.....it's the day that changed everything in my life
In one simple word......Cancer

It's been over a week since we heard the word......Cancer.
And we still have a million and one thoughts and questions going through our heads.
We were supposed to have some answers from the results of Alex's bone biopsy....In a way we did and didn't.
Here is what the doctors have ruled out:
Lymphoma
Leukemia
Langerhans Cell Hystocytosis
Some tests have come back inconclusive and some tests are still

being run.....so we wait for the results.
It's the waiting that is bothering me so much...
I like answers A.S.A.P.
I want to get our son on the road to treatment and recovery.
In a way, no news is good news...and the more the doctors' rule out, the better.
We are take each day as it comes and trying to keep things as normal as possible.

(Day 10)

April 4, 2011........Just another Monday to most people.
Not to me.....it's the day that changed everything in my life
In one simple word......Cancer

It's hard to believe it's been 10 days since we heard the word......Cancer.
Here's what we know and have learned since the beginning.......
Alex's pain is being controlled better with his pain meds.
He has tried to go to school this week......2 out of 3 days he had to come home early.
He knows what is going on and knows it's going to be a long battle to recovery.
Alex has truly become one of the bravest people I know.
Oncologists have done some tests and a bone biopsy. They now say there isn't a definitive diagnosis.

Everything is certainly looking and acting like cancer as originally discussed, but tests are all coming back negative.

Bone biopsy showed 90% healthy bone with 10% abnormal but not diagnostic.

Bones are definitely in some major trouble but they can't pinpoint the cells causing the trouble and afraid to start treatment until they know for sure what they are battling.

A neurosurgeon is now looking at the lesions on the back of his skull. They may possibly have to do another biopsy.

So we still just have to play the waiting game.......and that really sucks.

CHAPTER 3

(Day 21)

April 4, 2011........Just another Monday to most people.
Not to me.....it's the day that changed everything in my life
In one simple word......Cancer

It's hard to believe it's been 3 weeks......since we heard the word--Cancer
I haven't updated in a while because there hasn't been much to report.....and still isn't much.
Here is what we do know:
The doctors are having a hard time pin pointing exactly what type of cancer it is. They are now saying it could possibly be a type of lymphoma or leukemia. Again, they are still not sure.
The doctors don't want to start just any kind of cancer treatment. They

will be starting him on steroids to help with inflammation.
This Wednesday Alex is scheduled to have another biopsy...this time on the back of his head.
The first biopsy from his leg came back inconclusive.
Alex is also in a back brace...which he hates.
He knows he needs to wear it...it's to help the spine from compressing (more).
His pain meds have been doubled up to help control his pain better.
We thought we could control his pain enough for him to go to school.....he really does miss being there and his friends miss him not being there too.
Since he can only be comfortable sitting up for so long, he couldn't make it a full day.

So we have his homework coming home so he can keep up.
He's thrilled about that as you can imagine.
Emotionally he has good and bad days.......it's our job to make sure the good outweigh the bad.
I wish I could peek inside his mind to know exactly how he feels or what he is thinking.
This is a lot for an adult to go through.....let alone a child.
At times Alex can be very stoic......
I hope he isn't thinking this is a burden and doesn't want it to be for the rest of us...I hope he knows we are a team and all in this together.
I have learned my actions and feelings can make his feelings and frustration worse too.
Nancy, on more than one occasion, had to remind me to keep my feelings or frustrations in check or behind closed doors.
I thank God for Nancy.....she really has been the rock for me and the family.

And we can't thank all of you enough for the kind words, thoughts, prayers, and good vibes for our family....We are grateful for having all of you in our lives.

(Day 23)

April 4, 2011........Was just another Monday to most people.
Not to me.....it's the day that changed everything in my life
In one simple word......Cancer

Today's the day we were hoping answers would finally arrive.
Alex had his biopsy on the back of the skull......Pathology looked at the sample immediately after surgery.
All the doctors knew we wanted answers today.....well we got them.
It wasn't the answer we had hoped for.....best case scenario benign lesions and a disease called Langerhans Cell Histiocytosis.
Instead our world stopped.
Alex has been diagnosed with what they think is Stage 4 Malignant Sarcoma.
The doctors said treatments are going to be very aggressive... before

treatments can start several things are going to happen.
MRI, PET scan, brain scan, surgery for a port for chemo, lumbar puncture, and bone marrow aspiration will all be done in the next few days.
Needless to say we have a very scared boy and he has very scared parents.
Our goal is just to keep him comfortable and get the best care out there.
And I'll do whatever it takes to make sure it happens.
Nancy and I are very confident with the Oncologist Alex has...she's a straight shooter.
This is good for us....we don't want things sugarcoated.....even if it's something that might be hard to hear.
There is going to be plenty of sleepless nights ahead.
We just need to remain strong and be the rock for Alex to hold onto.
If I could ask one thing...in the prayers, thoughts, and good vibes,

could you please keep Courtney and Ryan in them too? They love their brother so much.
As Nancy told me today.....Take it one day at a time.

(Day 26)

April 4, 2011........Was just another Monday to most people.
Not to me.....it's the day that changed everything in my life
In one simple word......Cancer

The last few days have been very overwhelming... A 3 hour MRI and PET scan.
We are all starting to feel the strain of the battle...emotionally and physically.

Last night was a very scary night.....
For whatever reason...Alex had so much pain in his head and it overpowered him to the point he was unable to move....slurred his speech, and affected his eyesight.
He was rushed to Mount Clemens Regional Hospital......The treatment there was great!

They quickly got his pain under control.....And transferred him to Children's Hospital in Detroit.
For added excitement Alex did get his first ride in an ambulance.
The hardest thing as a parent is to see your child in pain....the worst part is feeling helpless in trying to comfort them.
He was admitted for the night at Children's for 2 reasons.....1st to observe him and 2nd we had to be at the hospital early the next morning for a brain scan.
This morning....pain was back under control and he was feeling good again.
So good in fact this afternoon we were able to play a little catch with a football while he sat in his wheelchair...and that made me feel good.
In the time we were at Children's we learned something....the Oncologist on duty told us his results from the biopsy on the back of the skull......the final diagnosis from Pathology is Lymphoma of the bone.

We know what we are battling now…..it's a small relief…..very small.

CHAPTER 4

(Day 49)

April 4, 2011........Was just another Monday to most people.
Not to me.....it's the day that changed everything in my life
In one simple word......Cancer

I have learned to take each day as it comes.....don't worry about yesterday and don't think about tomorrow.
Every day just runs together.
A lot has happened since the last time I posted 3 weeks ago.
Alex had 3 procedures done: a lumbar puncture, bone marrow biopsy, and he got his battle gear on.....a surgically implanted port.
Needless to say he wasn't in a very good mood.
The reality of things....HIT!!
Alex was admitted to the Oncology floor to begin his treatment.

96 hours of infused chemo therapy.....he was scared; I was scared, we were all scared.
This is where I put my faith in the hands of science to fix him.....and I place my hands together to pray God heals him...That says a lot.....I'm not the over religious type of guy...but I know what team I play on.
Alex handled the 1st round of chemotherapy like a champ...His room was filled daily with people who love and care about him.....And I think that's what got him through it.
He has 96 hours of chemo therapy every 21 days....it's aggressive and will put him on the road to recovery and regain his health much faster.
Alex has been home.....he has even been going to school for a half day at a time.
He has even taken his scooter and bike out for a spin or 2.....causing me more gray hair.
He's a kid....and I still have to let him be a kid when he feels like it.

We like things to be as normal as possible.
That's sometimes easier said than done......
The side effects of the chemo have begun to take place....from sores in his mouth to his hair falling out.
The hair falling out was hard.....it was something physically he/we could see.
In true Alex fashion he got upset....and then made jokes.
(I'm not allowed to say "wispy" anymore)
I was brushing his hair and it was falling across his forehead.   I told him "Your hair is so wispy"
He stood up looked me in the face and joked "Do you know how gay you sounded when you said Wispy"

I think the coolest thing to happen to Alex...was set up by his gym teacher (Mr. Marks) and 6th grade teacher (Ms. Bean)
They arranged to have Frank Zombo, a linebacker for the Super Bowl Champion Green Bay Packers,

come to the house and hangout with Alex and his buddies for a while.....autographs and smiles for everyone.
They even managed to play a little football.
IT WAS GREAT!!!
Alex played quarterback...Frank told him "Don't worry...I won't let anyone get you!"...Alex surprised everyone when he took off running with Frank Zombo as his blocker...poor kids didn't have a chance.
That was this past Saturday......The timing couldn't have been more perfect.
 As I write this Alex is back in the hospital....I'm actually looking at his hospital bed. He is the bravest person I know. I'm watching him sleep as the drugs that will fix him are working their way through his body again......21 days go by fast. This time we kind of know what to expect.....it takes a little bit of the scariness away.

Though after this round of treatment we will find out how well he is reacting to it.

I can't thank everyone enough for helping us through this time.......If the time ever comes and all you who have been the best friends and family members a person can have.... I will be as great to you as you all have been to me and my family.

CHAPTER 5

(Day 71)

April 4, 2011........Was just another Monday to most people.
Not to me.....it's the day that changed everything in my life
In one simple word......Cancer

Still taking life each day as it comes.
We are currently in round 3 of treatment....21 days goes by awfully quick.
This should be the half-way point of chemo treatments....There's some good news.
With each round of treatment my optimism grows that the medicines are doing what they are supposed to be doing.
Hopefully, I'm not just fooling myself into that kind of thinking.

Alex's pain has gone away quite a bit and he's not hunched over like before he started his treatments.
He still needs his wheelchair as his back gets tired and aches.

We've learned this time around NOTHING is routine....
After the last round of treatments Alex went in for a "routine" appointment in the Oncology clinic to check blood counts, they weren't were they should be...and he needed a blood transfusion,
It wasn't exactly routine.
Alex was less than thrilled.

In between this round and the next round of treatments, Alex is scheduled for a MRI.
Hopefully, we can see some improvement.

The doctor really isn't optimistic of seeing any changes in his bones because they take a long time to heal.
She said they would try.
It will be a 2-3 hour scan so he will have to be sedated :(He hates the sedation :(.

Chemo weeks are tough on everybody in my family...I think Courtney and Ryan feel like they're being left out because we spend so much time with Alex at the hospital and his doctor appointments....If they only knew how much they are on my mind.
This isn't easy for them either....I wish I could look into their minds to see exactly how they feel.
They all have grown up so much since April 4th.

After going through all this day after day and week after week...We all still find a way to smile...maybe not all the time but I'll still take any smile any time of the day.

Since all this started, I never knew so many people cared about my son and family.....I can never thank all of you enough for your kind words, love, prayers, and support.

CHAPTER 6

(Day 94)

April 4, 2011........Was just another Monday to most people.
Not to me.....it's the day that changed everything in my life
In one simple word......Cancer

My Hero is still battling.
Alex is currently in the middle of round 4 of his chemo treatments.
You would think by now all of us would be used to the routine.
But how can you get used to something you HATE!?
I think that's his motivation to win this battle.
He's not letting it get him down, his attitude amazes me.
I thought his hair loss would be discouraging and he would want to

hide it with hats, bandana's, or even shave it all off.
He has no problem going without those things...I keep asking him if he wants to shave it off.
His answer was greater than I would have imagined from a 12 year old boy.
"I don't want to shave it, when the last piece of hair falls out I'm going to save it in a plastic bag so it will remind me of the battle I fought and...WON!"
He had a couple of great days in between treatments....spent a lot of time with family, swimming, and even played a little basketball with the boys in the neighborhood...(That scared me).

Alex just wants to be one of the boys...he knows his limitations but doesn't want them to stop him.
A fall can break almost every bone in his body or he can wear himself down to the point of getting sick, which is why it scares me so much. We've been lucky. He has had no setbacks so far...everything has been going to schedule.
Way back in my mind...I keep waiting for the bottom to fall out...I hope it doesn't.

The next major test is his MRI scheduled for July 20th...this is when doctors will see if the treatments are doing what they are supposed to. It's a long MRI...roughly 3 hours; Alex will have to be sedated for it. Another thing he HATES.
But it's just another battle to get through.
Alex knows he isn't fighting this battle on his own...There's not a day that doesn't go by where he doesn't get words of encouragement from

friends, family, and people who don't even know him.
I think this is what has improved his attitude...And I can't thank everyone enough for their support.

(Day 112)

April 4, 2011........Was just another Monday to most people.
Not to me......it's the day that changed everything in my life
In one simple word......Cancer

It's hard to believe almost 4 months have passed.
So much has changed...
Alex walked into the Oncology clinic today...we usually wheel him in, but today he asked to leave the wheelchair in the van.
That's the biggest improvement we can see.
It looks like he is winning this battle!!
His pain is more tolerable and at times...not all.
That makes him feel like a normal kid again....which is just what he needs.
NORMAL!!

We did have a couple of great weeks in between treatments.
Had some family fun time to clear our heads...at the family cabin.
4 wheelers and beach bumming was just what the doctor ordered...kind of.
Actually she said rest and relaxation...But who really listens to doctors?
It gave us all a big break from reality...which is what we needed.
But as much as things change....some are still the same.
21 days have already passed and Alex is back in chemo treatment.
He wished chemo wecks went by as fast as the 2 weeks in between seem to.
We also got the results from his MRI...we wanted to see if there is any improvement.

The news wasn't as good as we have hoped for.
Looks like there could be a little bit more bone deterioration in his vertebrae and upper femur.

Not exactly what we wanted to hear as Alex enters his 5th round of treatment.
I wanted to see a marked improvement with his bones...but knowing his pain is under control is good enough for me...for now.
We'll take this small set back with a grain of salt knowing Alex is winning battles but still has a war to win.
Thank you all for your continued support, kind words, and encouragement...it means so much to me and my family.

CHAPTER 7

(Day 134)

April 4, 2011........Was just another Monday to most people.
Not to me.....it's the day that changed everything in my life
In one simple word......Cancer

This isn't going to be a typical update...it's a good news, bad news, and some venting.

All things considered, things are going pretty good.
Alex is using his wheelchair less and less, his legs and back are still getting tired and achy, but it's much better than it was in April.
His eyelashes and eyebrows are now starting to fall out from the chemo drugs. His hair never fell out completely and he is confident enough in himself to go out without a hat on to cover his wispy hair. It

doesn't bother him children try to get a look at him. It gives him a chance to tell them he's fighting against cancer. It's the adults who make him angry when they stare. Can't say I blame him for getting angry. It pisses me off too!!

We had a great couple of weeks in between treatments, a 4-H fair, 2 concerts (Rascal Flatts & Kid Rock), a trip to the zoo, and few days of just goofing around the house with Courtney, Ryan, and friends.
He's still a kid and it's still summer!!

This week is supposed to be Alex's last round of in-patient chemotherapy...It can't get over soon enough.
We hope this is still true...that it is his last round, but right now we feel like we are being left in limbo.

His doctor has been out of town for most of the summer, there has been only one MRI done since he's been in treatment, and it didn't come back favorable.
So our biggest question is NOW WHAT??!!
I hate the not knowing.
When are they going to schedule another PET scan or do more evaluations on the deterioration of his bones?
It's hard to get those answers when the doctor isn't around to ask

The questions mount daily.

Every minute we are here at Children's Hospital we become more and more disenchanted with the place.
We've spent time second guessing ourselves to why we didn't go to Mott's Children Hospital or even St. Jude's.
We felt we were in good hands with the doctors...but as time has gone on the feeling leaves us with every

doctor's appointment and hospital stay.
Twice they've switched Alex's chart with someone else's. This could be very dangerous for both children, not to mention a violation of HIPPA laws.
Luckily we caught it both times before any meds were given.
The wait time has become unimaginable...we make appointments for 10 a.m. and they don't start pushing chemo until 10 p.m.....What the hell takes 12 hours to get the chemo drugs??

I know how it makes me and Nancy feel....Our stress level is through the roof!!
Not to mention we can only imagine how Alex feels while waiting.
Maybe we are expecting too much or set our expectations too high for a hospital ranked in the Top 10 in the country.
We know we aren't in this alone...many of you have been there with an ear to listen, a shoulder to

lean on, and so much more, we truly know some amazing people and are blessed to have you all in our lives.

(Day 148)

April 4, 2011........Was just another Monday to most people.
Not to me.....it's the day that changed everything in my life
In one simple word......Cancer

A small sigh of relief....
Alex finished what we hope is his last round of in-patient chemotherapy on August 20th.
His resolve has been tremendous through this fight, I've never seen a 12 year old so mentally tough.
Hardly anything has brought him down...he took each treatment as a challenge. A fighter he arose to the challenge round after round.
He is our Hero!!
Just in time for school to start.
The doctors gave him the go ahead to go back to school...I think he's the only 12 year old to actually be excited for school to start.

The only thing bumming him out about school is he won't be able to be in gym class.
Sports are a big part of his life. He probably misses this more than he misses his hair.
He's going to take each day as it comes.
School brings a sense of normalcy to our house too.

Now we have to wait...Again
You would think with everything Alex has been through our anxiety would go away, but it's probably higher than ever now.
The waiting and not knowing drives it higher every day.
Alex has a re-evaluation scheduled for the end of September.
It will be the same tests and scans he had when first diagnosed...MRI, brain scan, spine scan, and PET scan.
We pray every day the chemo has done what it was supposed to do.
After all the tests and scans are done...

I would give everything I have just to hear the words "ALL CLEAR!

"CHAPTER 8

The Hardest Question to Answer......

"How's Alex doing?"

It's the same question over and over when some sees me or my wife Nancy. We appreciate the thought and sentiment behind the question. People genuinely care about our son. Over time it gets to the point when you don't want to answer the question anymore. It's the same generic answer every time...."He's doing fine." What else could we answer or should we answer. Sure we could answer with...his hair fell out, he has sores in his mouth, he's tired, he's weak, or he's been throwing up. Those are the real life answers; those are the things happening when someone is battling cancer and undergoing chemotherapy. Some people want to hear those answers...we were very reluctant to give them. When we gave those answers, we would get sympathy. To be honest…we didn't want someone to tell us how sorry they felt for us, what Alex is going through, and what our family was going through. We already knew. More than anything we appreciated their support in the fight, the prayers for healing, the positive vibes, and thoughts to give us strength. We wouldn't be where we are today without everyone being there for us.

We had our own "How's Alex Doing?" questions. Those questions were for the doctors. Those questions were the hardest to ask and even harder to wait for the answers. Yes I said wait…because that's what you do…WAIT. I hated waiting, I wanted answers…NOW! It's our 12 year old son we were asking about. Understandably getting the right answers takes time…tests take time, lab results take time, getting a diagnosis takes time. Waiting for a diagnosis was the longest time of our life. I think half my hair went gray in the three weeks we waited from the first time we heard our son had a form of cancer to the diagnosis of Large B Cell Lymphoma of the Bone. At least we finally had an answer!

All that answer did was brought more questions. A ton more questions...We just hoped the doctors had the answers.

Q. Now what?
A. We fix him!
Q. Chemotherapy or radiation?
A. Chemotherapy...aggressive chemotherapy
Q. How soon?
A. Right away!
Q. How long will it last?
A. Six rounds of 96 hours of infused chemotherapy at a time
Q. How will you know the therapy will work?
A. We don't...time will tell.

All those questions make the question of "How's Alex doing?" seem so trivial…but so much easier to answer. The difference between our questions and everyone else's…we NEEDED answers, everyone else WANTED answers. It's frustrating waiting for answers…whether you want to hear them or not. The longer we waited for answers the more our, or at least my mind wandered to the "What if?" questions, and honestly that's really not a place you want your mind to wander to. I really started to get a feeling for the Tom Petty song "Waiting is the Hardest Part"…it played over and over in my head. Thankfully all our questions are answered….in due time, when they could be answered with decisive answers. Persistence does pay off. Something my wife and I learned in the year we fought the good fight against our son's cancer, and could pass on to others: it's never stop asking questions. Question everything and everybody…from the doctors and nurses in the oncology clinic to the doctors and nurses in the hospital. It could actually save a life!

CHAPTER 9

"Dad Why Did God Choose Me to be Sick?"
(Day 140)

Alex asked me this question...I didn't know how to answer it...Many of you gave me great answers...I thought who would be better to help me answer the question than one of our church's Pastors, and here is the response I got...It helped me greatly!

James,
The most heart breaking part of our fallen humanity is the trials and troubles come seemingly without rhyme or reason on us way too often.
In the midst of evil; we know God is going to bring miracles through it as he promises to work good out of all things. I know He says, He will never give us more than

we can handle; I am sure there are days when it doesn't feel like it, yet He says it. Hearing Miss Bean talk about Alex and how He brings smiles to other kid's faces at the hospital and how your family is being a blessing through the midst of this tells me God is working good through this like only He can do through you all. I know God says He is with you and I hope you have experienced this. I know He is stronger than Satan, the one that has caused all evil, and Jesus has Alex's back. We know Jesus has kicked Satan's butt so that we will all have heaven, the place where things are the way they were meant to be, the perfect place that lasts forever. On this side of eternity, I am praying Jesus wins this battle. I don't think I can say God caused Alex's cancer. I know He knew it was going to happen when He created Alex. I would also reaffirm there is nothing Alex did or didn't do that caused his cancer.

I wish I knew more about God and I wish He would wipe evil out completely, but for now I believe God is not done with Alex and He is definitely using Alex through his illness to share His love with the hurting and to give hope. I pray God gives Alex an extra measure of courage and strength as he continues to fight against cancer, also for you as his parents.
One thing I read from a man named C.S. Lewis, whose wife died at an early age, is God shouts in our pain. I pray God is very evident to you guys through Alex's sickness. I pray you know how much God's heart is breaking for you as your son suffers. He does understand.

I hope this answers the question somewhat; it is hard to communicate this via e-mail. Let me say this, I know you, hundreds of people, and we at Trinity are praying for him and over him but if you guys would ever like us Pastor's and/or Elders to come and pray over Alex we would be honored.

You are a great dad... I know God is proud of you in the way you love your son...
Pastor Justin

CHAPTER 10

(Day 191)

April 4, 2011........Was just another Monday to most people.
Not to me.....it's the day that changed everything in my life
In one simple word......Cancer

It's hard to believe it's been 6 months since this battle began....every day is still a fight, and it's a good fight he can win.
So much has changed....
Alex is done with chemotherapy....for now and we hope for good.
He has handled it remarkably well...blood counts have stayed normal which is a good thing considering his immune system will be suppressed for the next year or so.
Every cough and sneeze puts us on more alert for fevers and anything else can send him to the hospital,

luckily for me, Nancy doesn't panic over these things.
I do!
He's been going to school when he can...he gets run down fast so there's days he just can't make it. For the past month he's been fighting off bronchitis and ear infections, like everything else he just battles against it.
Alex did give up on one fight though...he decided his hair was getting too thin...so he made the decision to shave it.
I had the honor of doing it for him...I had to hold back the tears while doing so...True to what he said early on, he kept all the hair in a plastic bag and put in a keepsake box to remind him of this battle.

Alex is now in the re-evaluation stage...all the scans, tests, and x-rays all over again...just hoping for better results.
The 1st scan was a PET scan...probably one of the most important scans.

It came back with good news...no uptake in the bones means he is responding to treatment (breathe a sigh of relief)...but if they look hard enough they can always find something... a small spot the size of a pea on his lung...just something to keep an eye on.
Had a new MRI done on his brain and spine....NO LYMPHOMA in his brain.(Breath another sigh of relief)...The MRI of his spine showed no progression of the disease...but no regression either...so it seems the chemotherapy has stopped it and this is great news...But the question is..
Now what?
I guess we wait for the doctors' full evaluation...And I HATE waiting.
I want answers to make my boy better...but with everything he has been through as well as our family, I think we'll take what we have right now.
Just prior to posting this Alex looked at it and asked
"Has it really been 191 days?"

(Day 211)

April 4, 2011........Was just another Monday to most people.
Not to me.....it's the day that changed everything in my life
In one simple word......Cancer

It's been almost 7 months.....so much has changed...for the better....FINALLY SOME GOOD NEWS!!
From what the doctors have said....it looks like Alex is on the road to recovery.
After all the re-evaluations have been done...
The PET scan showed there is NO malignant activity.
That's a big sigh of relief!!
The MRI showed there is still widespread bone damage and it's just going to take time to heal.
This serves as a reminder we aren't quite out of the woods yet....but good enough to have Alex's port removed since he won't need any

more chemotherapy...at least for now.

I say for now.... because there is a chance the lymphoma cells could become active again.

Most lymphoma cases have a recurrence rate of 30-35%...being Alex's type of lymphoma is so rare the doctors couldn't even guess what the chance of recurrence could be....so we are keeping our fingers crossed.

If it does come back, a bone marrow transplant will be done.

We already met with the transplant team to prepare us for such an event. They are also starting the process of match testing.

We know Alex still has a long road ahead of him...and we hope the worst is behind him.

Alex looks so good these days...his hair is coming back in, eyebrows and lashes have almost grown back completely.

He doesn't have the chemo face anymore.

Now if we could just get rid of his damn cough....his immune system is so low it takes forever to get rid of any cold, sniffles, or whatever else is out there.

You are all proof the power of prayer works!! We appreciate you all for keeping us in your prayers and thoughts.
We can't thank you enough!!

CHAPTER 11

My Hero......By Courtney Craven (Day 221)

A hero is someone who is strong; someone who is brave, and that's why Alex, my brother, is my hero. Alex is 12 years old and normally a very active boy. But, he was diagnosed with Stage 4 Lymphoma of the bone.
Cancer has brought my family together, not only physically, but also emotionally. We stand by each other through everything. My Family's motto is "No One Fights Alone"
Alex truly is the toughest and strongest little boy I know.

All the generous donations and gifts people have given us is more than anyone could even imagine! The love and prayers that have been done is truly amazing! Miracles DO happen.

Every day the best thing to do is smile, laugh, and look at each day with your head held high.
Having cancer is a very scary thing to think about, being that a 12 year old has it (cancer), is even scarier. Alex is currently a 7th grader and is looking forward to playing soccer and basketball again.
Every day I thank God for the family I have.

God doesn't pick people who aren't strong enough to handle something as strong as cancer....God has a plan for everyone and this is His plan.
Exodus 14:13 "Do not be afraid"

CHAPTER 12

(Day 264)

April 4, 2011........Was just another Monday to most people.
Not to me.....it's the day that changed everything in my life
In one simple word......Cancer

The more things change....the more they stay the same.
MRI's, PET scans, and bone surveys....are the ways they are monitoring Alex's condition.
Most recently Alex had a PET scan, which is the most important test because it shows the hot spots (disease process), and this time around it's more good news....although there is still some disease process there, it's minimal. The doctors rate it on a scale of 0-10 to see if further chemotherapy or a bone marrow transplant is required,

anything over 5 or over would be a Yes....Alex is at a 2.9....So as of right now it's a big NO!!!!

This is the best Christmas present we could have asked for!!

We know Alex isn't out of the woods yet...his bones are still weak and fragile. We know anything can happen to send us back to the hospital...but he's smiling, doesn't complain of pain, and just wants to be as normal as he can be.

Alex has been blessed with some of the best friends he could ask for...they are the best support group... I have the proof in the form of a text message bill...Thank God for unlimited texting!!

Our families, friends, and more... have picked up our motto of "No one Fights Alone".....we too have been blessed with having each and every one of you in our lives as our support group...offering a shoulder to cry or lean on to help us when we ask for help.

You have all been there for us...And we can never show our appreciation or thank you all enough!!

THANK YOU FOR YOUR CONTINUED THOUGHTS AND PRAYERS WE HOPE YOU ALL HAVE A BLESSED HOLIDAY SEASON

CHAPTER 13

11 Things 2011 Taught Me
December 31ˢᵗ 2011

11. This year I learned to expect the unexpected.
10. This year I learned the meaning of strength in numbers...thanks to family, friends, and strangers.
9. This year I learned to hate something with every feeling I have.
8. This year I witnessed the power of prayers.
7. This year I learned that nothing is too trivial.
6. This year I learned what it feels like to be inspired.
5. This year I learned to love more than I ever thought I could.
4. This year I've learned how to make sacrifices.
3. This year the words "hope" and "dreams" took on a new meaning.
2. This year I learned how strong my family is.

1. This year...is a year that will never be forgotten.

CHAPTER 14

(10 Months)

April 4, 2011....Just another Monday to most people.
Not to me....it was the day that changed everything in my life.
In one simple word....Cancer.

What a difference time makes.
I still have the feeling of uncertainty ....though it grows less and less every day, since hearing the word "remission" at his last doctor's appointment on January 11th. Although I prefer to use the words "cautiously optimistic" since it hasn't even been a year since he was diagnosed.
BIG SIGH OF RELIEF!!
It's such a relief to know Alex doesn't need to be on any kind of medications, and he hasn't had any chemotherapy since the end of August. His blood counts remain

normal and stable...all positive signs!!
He just needs to be patient for his bones to heal, this is going to take time.... thankfully we have the time.

Alex has fought the battles and it looks like he may have won the war. He's regaining his strength every day and getting back to the boy he was before ....it's truly remarkable. Now we just pray he stays this way. I don't think I can handle it if he took steps backwards...
But the "what if" will always be there in the back of my head as we look forward.
And that's what we're doing...Looking FORWARD!!

Next week...Alex gets to go on his wish trip through Rainbow Connection of Michigan...his dream and wish was to swim with dolphins and this is exactly what he gets to do at Discovery Cove in Orlando....as well as Disney World, Sea World, and Universal Studios....this trip couldn't happen without the Knights of Columbus council in Fraser, MI...They chose to sponsor Alex and we couldn't thank them enough for doing so.

All of you have been on this roller coaster with me and my family for almost a year...with shoulders to lean on, words of encouragement, prayers, and so much more...I don't think we could have gotten through this without you and I can never thank you enough...I am truly humbled.

CHAPTER 15
1 YEAR LATER!

(Day 365)

April 4, 2011....Just another Monday to most people.
Not to me....it was the day that changed everything in my life.
In one simple word....Cancer.

It's hard to believe it's been a year since I heard the word that would change my family's life.
It still doesn't make it any easier to say the word...cancer.
Everything in my life up to that point is a blur....But I can remember exactly what has happened every day since then, like it just happened.

I still remember my phone ringing at work at 3:03 pm on the afternoon of Monday April 4th, 2011

It was the doctor's office telling me they need me and my wife to come to the office as soon as we can.
I thought it was weird they called me...the doctor always calls Moms they never call Dad...they couldn't get a hold of her.
I tried to put it off until the next day...I knew Nancy was just starting her nursing clinical...at all places Children's Hospital in Detroit on the Oncology floor. The doctor's office insisted I get a hold of her and get to the office....somehow I did...with a million and one thoughts going through my head (this was actually my Facebook post as I left my office).
I knew it wasn't going to be good.

We waited for what seemed like an eternity waiting for the doctor....

I know the doctor explained what Alex's bones looked like and it was a type of cancer...but my brain popped at hearing the word...she could have just stopped talking.

That was then...it's behind us...Today is NOW and that's what we live for.

Alex has had 2 PET scans since his treatments have ended in August...both have showed no malignant activity.
No signs of cancer...the treatments worked...his positive attitude worked...he's NOW in remission!!
There have been no setbacks in his recovery and no bone breaks which are amazing for as brittle as his bones were and still are.

It's hard to tell he had to fight the battle, he's energetic, he's sassy, he has hair...and he's alive in every sense of the word, he has an almost an invincibility quality to him.

He knows there's nothing he can't do.
And that is AWESOME to know.

(Day 510)

Monday April 4th, 2011
Just another Monday to most people
Not to me…it's the day that changed everything in my life.
In 1 simple word…Cancer

It seems like a long time since I first wrote those words…but it feels like yesterday….
But today is Monday August 27th, 2012

1year ago…marked the last day of chemotherapy for Alex….he completed 6 rounds of intense therapy….96 hours at time. Those 6 rounds seemed like forever to get through…while this past year felt like it flew by. Everyday seemed like just like it was yesterday.
In the past year Alex has made up for lost time…

He was a fighter….now he's a survivor!!

Back to being the active boy he always was, he has a zest for life again and living it like there's no tomorrow.
He's found a new way to cause me gray hair...and I'll take it.
Riding his bike...I wish it was just simply riding it...that wouldn't worry me so much.
It's the tricks, the grinding, the jumping....there's no trick he won't try or a jump too high.
Every day it's a new bump, bruise or scrape...thankfully nothing broken.

He's made new friends because of it...on any given day it can look like a bike gang in my driveway.
None of his new friends were aware of what he's been through in the past year....
That was until one day noticed the scar on the back of Alex's head, and asked about
I overheard Alex explain to him...how and why he had the scar on the back of his head.

He didn't shy away from telling his story...and that surprised me...because he doesn't talk much about the past year too much.

And quite honestly...I hope he never has to tell a story like that again!

Chapter 16

Robby Atherton Foundation Speech on 8/20/12

"It was 1 year ago that I met Bryan Atherton and members of the Robby Atherton Foundation. I remember it clearly... I was here....my son Alex and my wife Nancy were down at Children's Hospital. It was Alex's last week and last round of chemotherapy....he was about to have his sixth round of therapy...the final 96 hours we hoped we would be spending in the hospital.

Alex was diagnosed with cancer on Monday April 4th 2011.... Lymphoma of the bone to be exact...it attacked 90% of the bones in his body It was the day that changed everything in our life. Family, friends, strangers, and Alex's determination...got us through to win this battle and I'm happy to say....we did it!! Alex has been declared in remission since March!!!

Cancer is a horrible disease as many as us know all too well...we also know it brings out the best in people...having strangers become friends.

Bryan Atherton...was one of those strangers. Somehow he heard about Alex....to this day I'm not sure how. But I'm sure glad he did! A year ago...The Robby Atherton Foundation chose to help my family with a very generous donation. When I was presented with an envelope...I was at a loss for words.

This year I asked if I could come back to say a few words....but mainly to say THANK YOU!! For caring and sharing Robby's spirit for life... sponsoring wish trips for children with life threatening illnesses through Rainbow Connection....helping families financially, and for helping an entire community like you have with the Robby Atherton Memorial Basketball courts at Mae Stecker Park.

Every person here today...and everyone that attend all of the fundraisers for Robby, truly are amazing people.

Thank you...thank you for turning tragedy into triumph!!"

For more information about the Robby Atherton Foundation...Please visit:

robbyathertonfoundation.org

Chapter 17

2011...A Year in Pictures

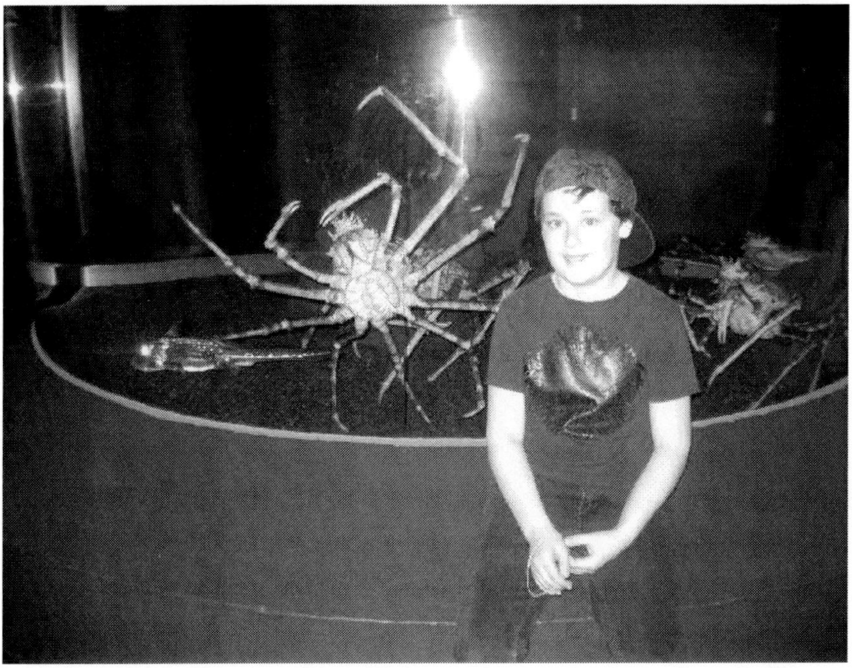

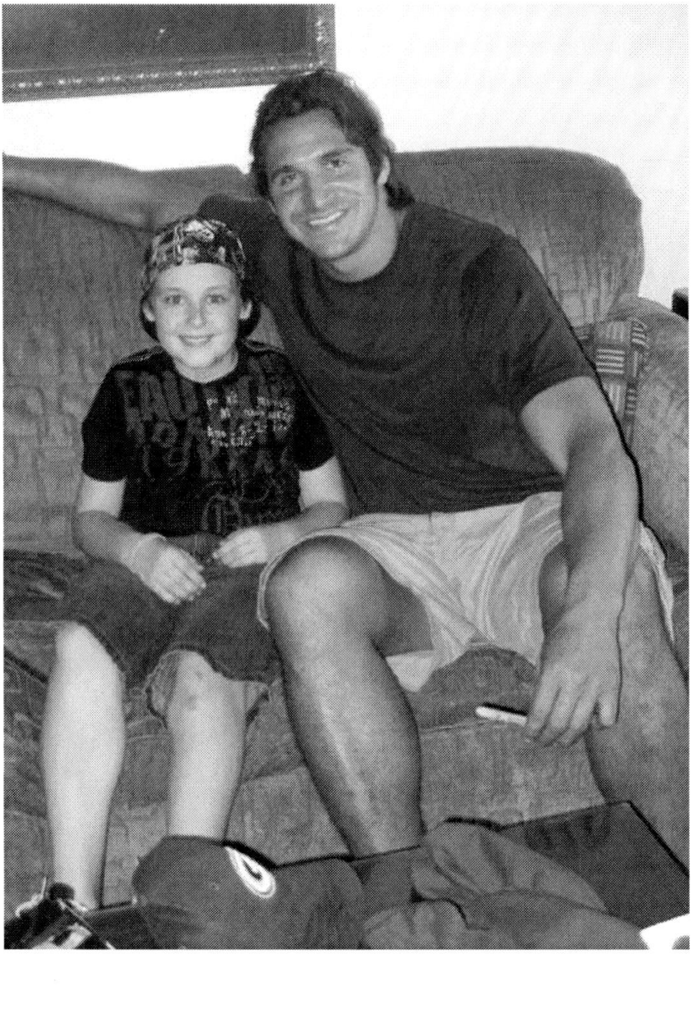

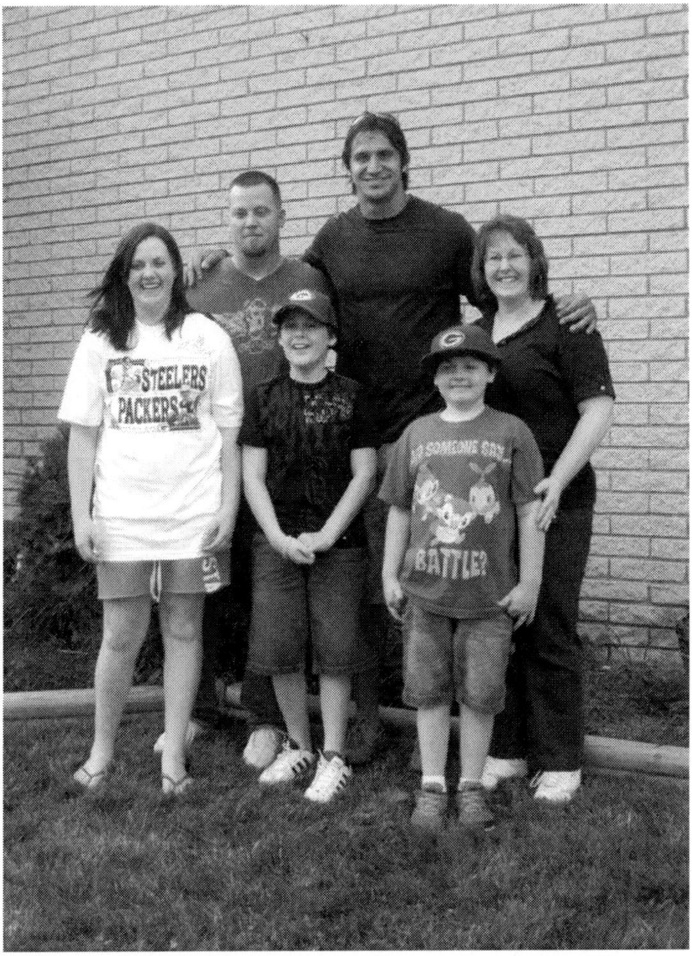
STEELERS
PACKERS
BATTLE?

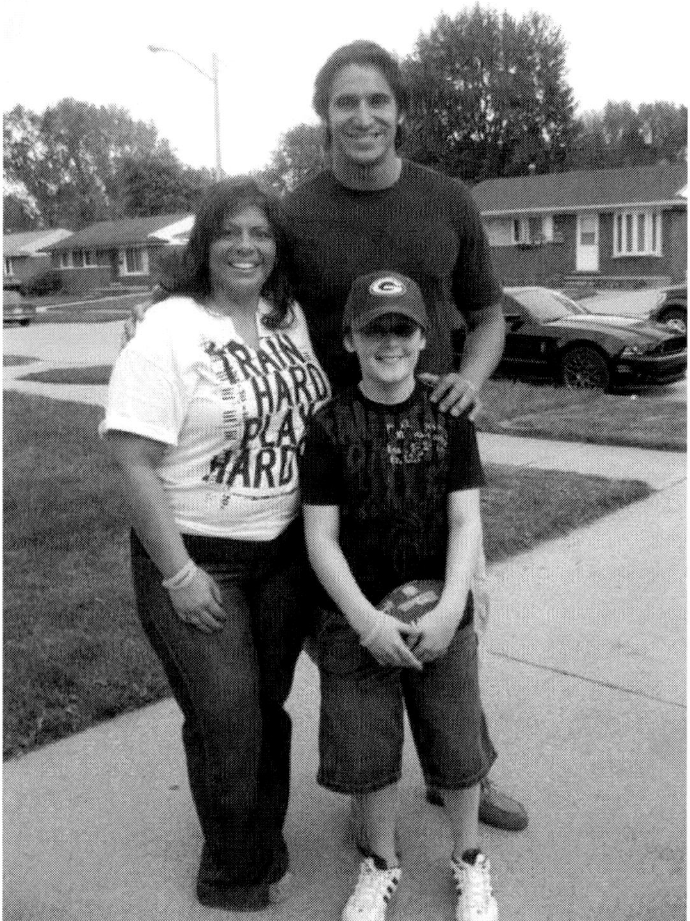
TRAIN
HARD
PLA
HARD

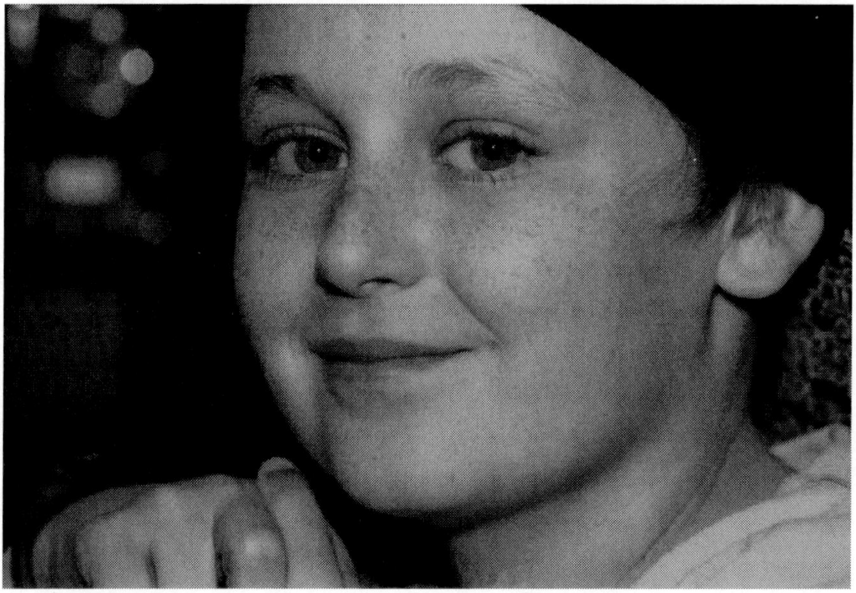

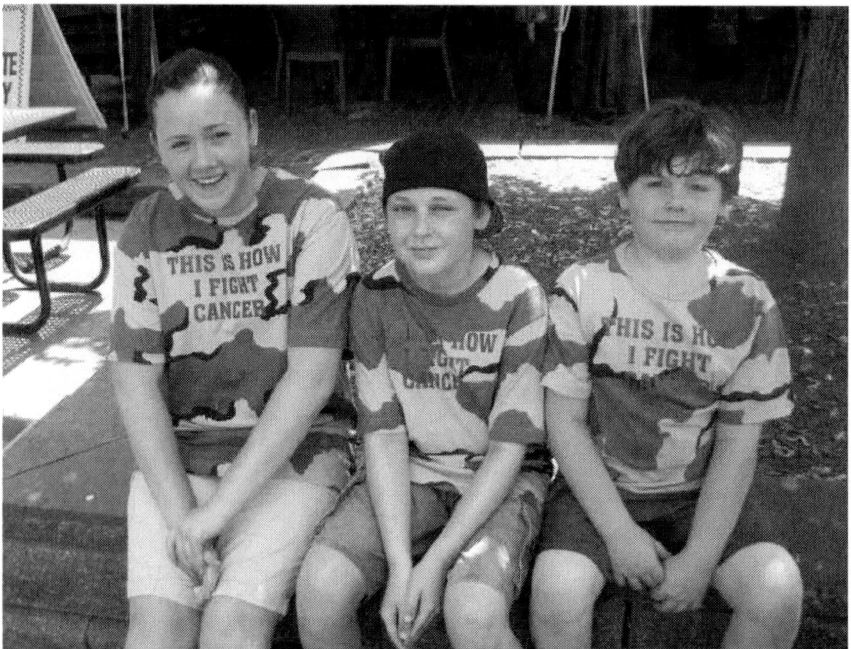
THIS IS HOW
I FIGHT
CANCER
I FIGHT

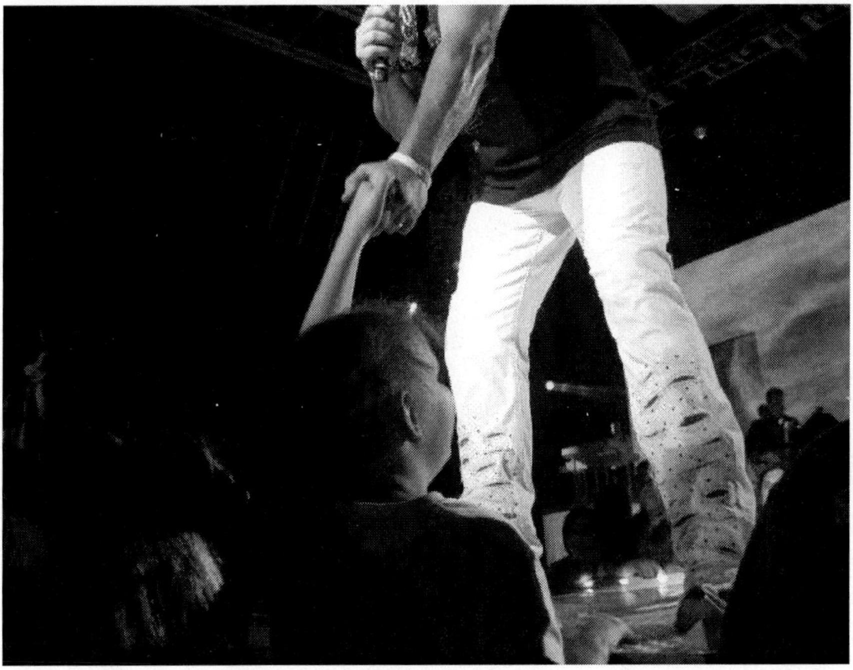

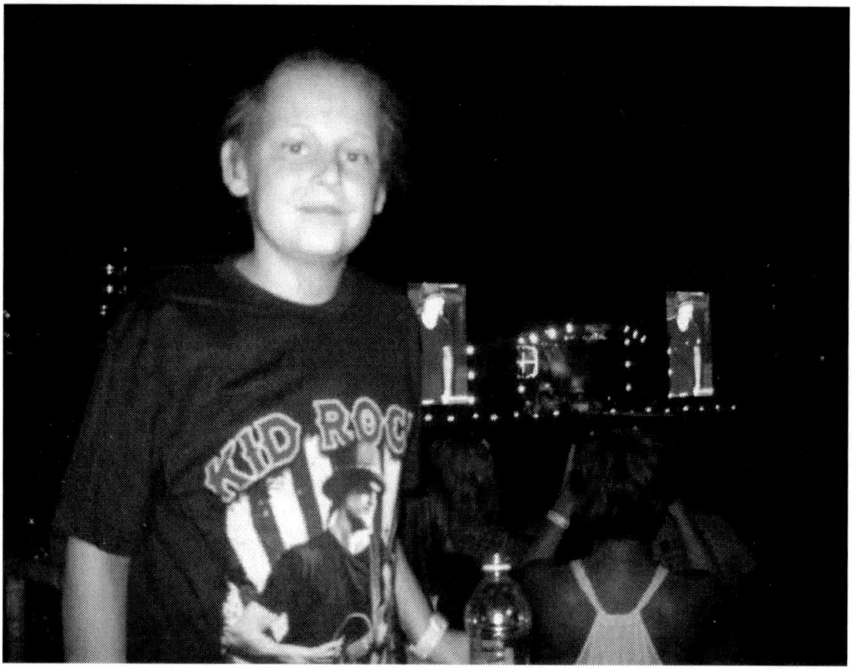
KID ROC

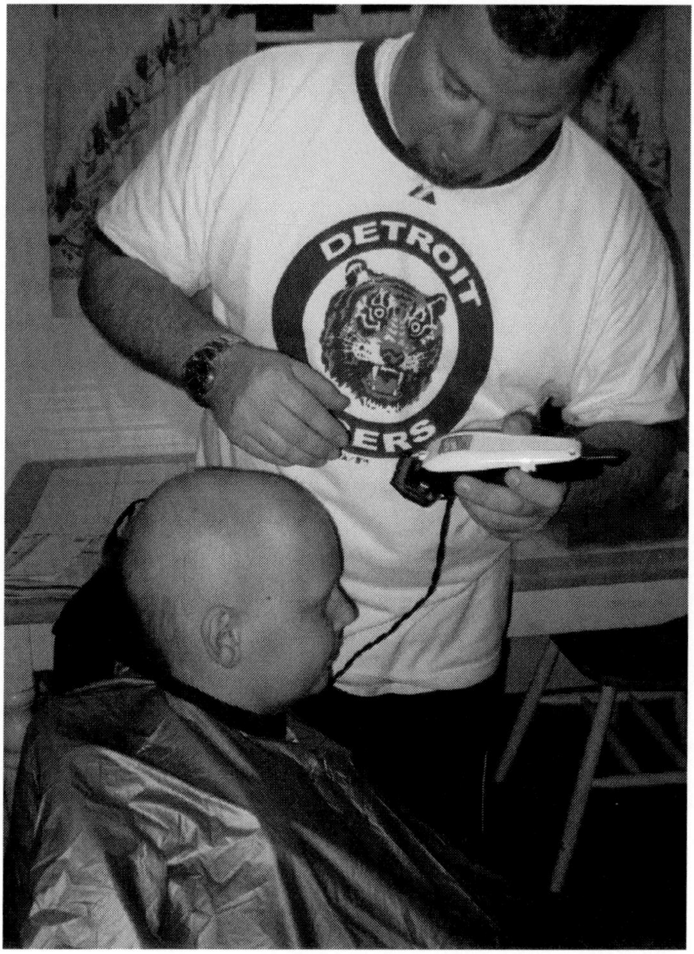
DETROIT

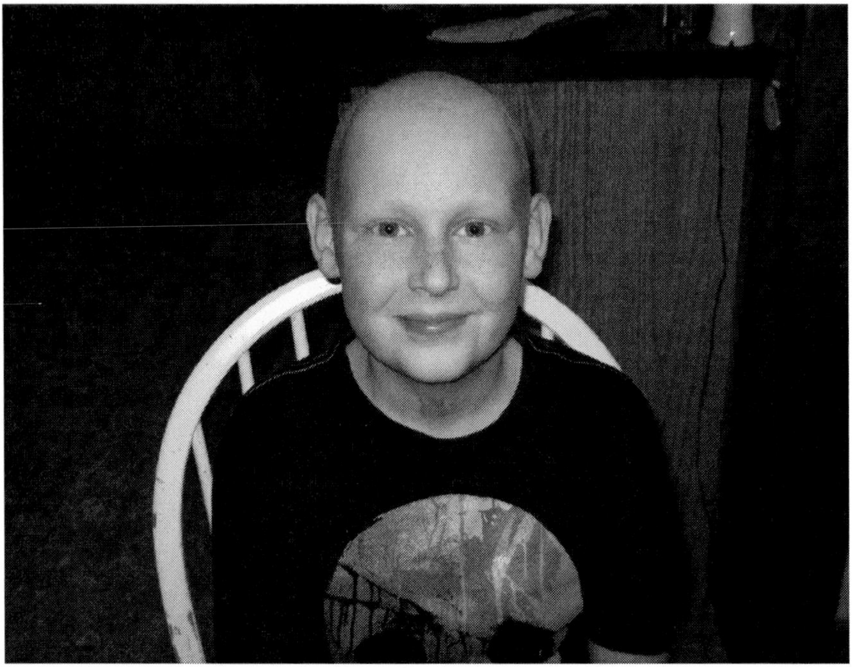

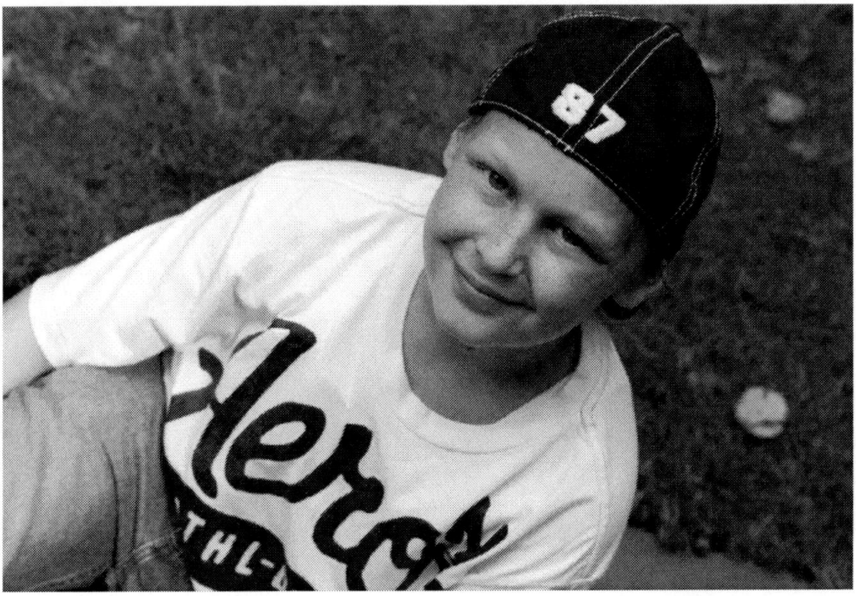
87

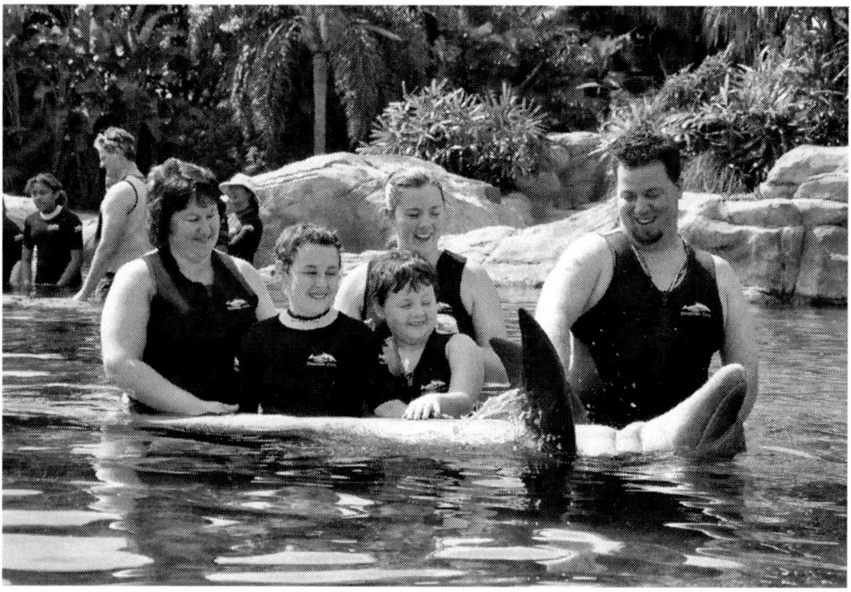

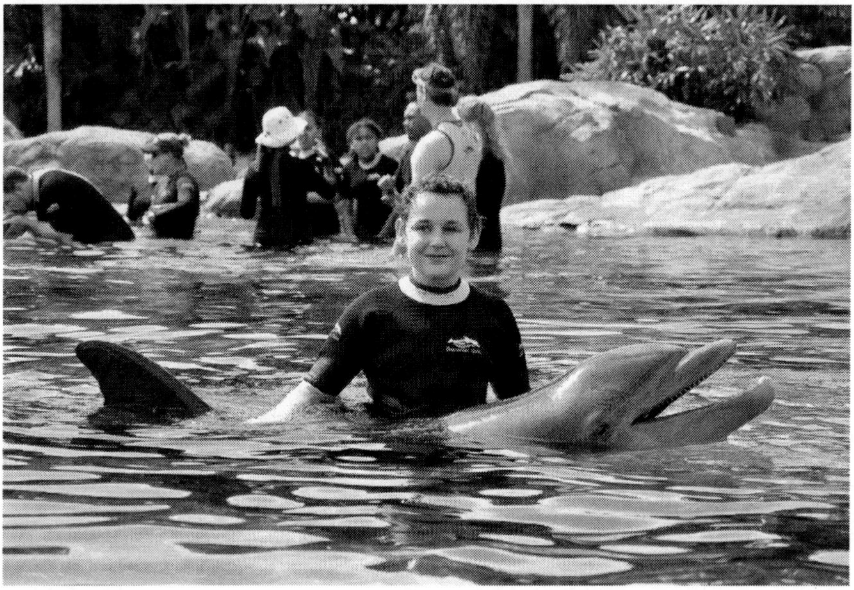

About the Author

James Craven is a stand-up comedian, husband and father of 3. He also is the creator/writer behind the Facebook dad advice page Dadisms and the Father of the Year web series. He uses his family life experiences to entertain the masses throughout the Mid-West. When not writing for his comedic web projects, Craven is actively involved with Cancer organizations and charities. His philosophy of making people laugh at themselves, him, life or whatever is what has helped him through his son's recent battle with stage 4 Lymphoma of the bone. Learning that inspiration can come from anywhere, he uses his daily life to make others laugh even in the rough times.

For updates and/or a good laugh check out:
lovecopingandcompassion.wordpress.com,
Facebook/dadisms, or
Facebook.com/cravencomedy.
Twitter.com/cravencomedy

A Note From The Author:

Cancer has touched just about everyone I know in some form or another. I never thought it would touch so close to my heart.

Monday, April 4th, 2011 was the hardest day of my life...it changed everything and every thought I have about life. It was the day I had to tell my 12 year old son he had cancer.

The rollercoaster of emotions since that day has been non-stop. I knew I would have to remain strong for him and not frighten him anymore. I would have to keep my feelings and emotions inside. I knew it wasn't going to be healthy for my frame of mind and I have to get them out...somehow.

I decided to put my thoughts, emotions, and feelings down on paper. I was keeping a chronicle to capture the" in the moment" thoughts I have had throughout the year since my son's diagnosis of Stage 4 Large B Cell Lymphoma of the bone.

It hasn't been easy...there have been a lot of tears, uncertainty, anger, laughs, love, and happiness as I write. In all honesty, I never thought to share my thoughts with the world...until I realized how much it got me through the bad, good, and great times.

This story was from the journal I kept every time we were in the hospital or doctor's office with Alex. Father's get a bad rap for holding in emotions and not knowing how to show them. I want to let parents know, especially fathers, you are not alone in your feelings when your child or loved one is faced with a life threatening illness such as cancer. My kids have seen me laugh and they laughed with me, I smile at them and they smile back, they've seen me angry and want to know why, most importantly...they've seen me cry and they've cried with me. Let them see who you are...

You're a father...your son's first hero...and your daughter's first love

Posted May 2012 on Twitter

A year ago I was pushing my son in a wheelchair...Just watched him run by the window

#KickedCancersAss